The "Me" I Am
Motivational Activity Book

Book 1

This motivational activity book belongs to

....

LIFE IS
TOUGH
BUT SO
AM I

Self Care Daily Routine

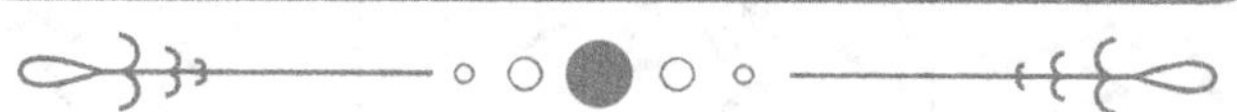

Letting Go of Negative thoughts

We all get negative thoughts – we just need to learn to
change them for positive thoughts.

Negative thought

What triggered this thought?

How did this thought make you feel?

What you might say if a friend expressed these negative thoughts?

What positive thought can you think of to replace the negative one?

Happy Memory Clouds

Fill out these clouds as you think of happy memories.
Use them when your emotions become too much.

What were you doing?

Where were you?

Who was there?

What could you hear?

What could you smell?

Grounding Yourself

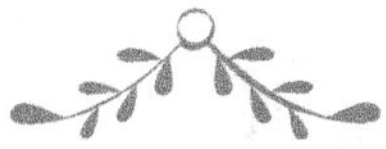

What is your name?...

Where are you

Words that describe yur space

Who is with you? What are they doing?

Words that describe your feelings

What do you hear?

What do you see?

What can you smell?

What can you touch?

When you are calm, set an intention.

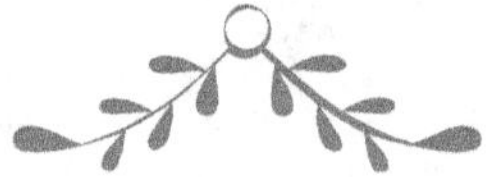 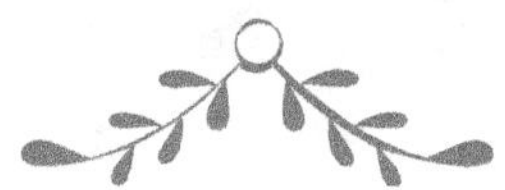

A Safe Space

Title of space...

Sketch your safe space here	Words that describe your space

Sounds	
Sights	
Smells	
Textures	
Who is present	

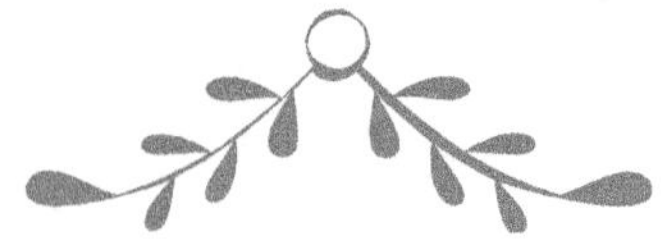

Body Scan

Today's date.............................   Time....................

Where are you?...

Head and Face

Neck and Shoulders

Back

Chest

Stomach

Arms

Legs

Whole body sensations

Sensations

warm – cold – soft – hard – breeze – damp – dry
tense – strong – taut – numb – tingling – tickling – muscle
slender – fragile - pressure – throbbing – blocked – pulse
stabbing – quivering - nauseous – shaking – aching – breathless
wired – anxious - soothed – relaxed – comfortable

Finger Labyrinth

Use your finger to slowly trace a path to the center of the labyrinth

Breathe calmly and slowly as you focus.
When you reach the center, draw a long deep breath or two.

Then trace your path back to the outside
Repeat until you feel more focused and calm.

Focus Words

Breathe - Peace - Relax - Tranquility - Serenity - Calm - Space - Beauty
Love - Wonder - Kindness - Light - Happiness - Joy - Warmth

I CAN DO IT

Self Care Daily Routine

Letting Go of Negative thoughts

We all get negative thoughts – we just need to learn to change them for positive thoughts.

Negative thought

What triggered this thought?

How did this thought make you feel?

What you might say if a friend expressed these negative thoughts?

What positive thought can you think of to replace the negative one?

Happy Memory Clouds

Fill out these clouds as you think of happy memories.
Use them when your emotions become too much.

What were you doing?

Where were you?

Who was there?

What could you hear?

What could you smell?

Grounding Yourself

What is your name?..

Where are you

Words that describe yur space

Who is with you? What are they doing?

Words that describe your feelings

What do you hear?

What do you see?

What can you smell?

What can you touch?

When you are calm, set an intention.

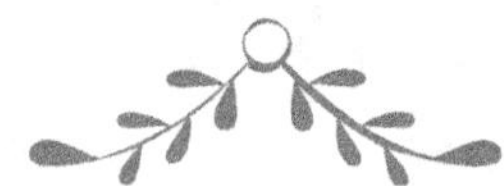

A Safe Space

Title of space...

Sketch your safe space here	Words that describe your space

Sounds	
Sights	
Smells	
Textures	
Who is present	

Body Scan

Today's date............................   Time....................

Where are you?...

Head and Face

Neck and Shoulders

Back

Legs

Chest

Stomach

Arms

Whole body sensations

Sensations

warm – cold – soft – hard – breeze – damp – dry
tense – strong – taut – numb – tingling – tickling – muscle
slender – fragile - pressure – throbbing – blocked – pulse
stabbing – quivering - nauseous – shaking – aching – breathless
wired – anxious - soothed – relaxed – comfortable

Finger Labyrinth

Use your finger to slowly trace a path to the center of the labyrinth

Breathe calmly and slowly as you focus.
When you reach the center, draw a long deep breath or two.

Then trace your path back to the outside
Repeat until you feel more focused and calm.

Focus Words

Breathe - Peace - Relax - Tranquility - Serenity - Calm - Space - Beauty
Love - Wonder - Kindness - Light - Happiness - Joy - Warmth

I AM
FEARLESS

Self Care Daily Routine

Letting Go of Negative thoughts

We all get negative thoughts – we just need to learn to
change them for positive thoughts.

Negative thought

What triggered this thought?

How did this thought make you feel?

What you might say if a friend expressed these negative thoughts?

What positive thought can you think of to replace the negative one?

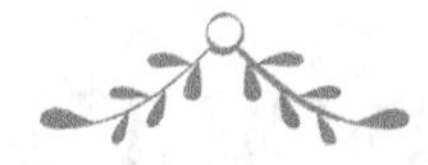

Happy Memory Clouds

Fill out these clouds as you think of happy memories.
Use them when your emotions become too much.

What were you doing?

Where were you?

Who was there?

What could you hear?

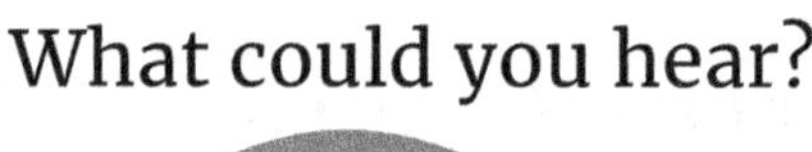

What could you smell?

Grounding Yourself

What is your name?......................................

Where are you

Words that describe yur space

Who is with you? What are they doing?

Words that describe your feelings

What do you hear?

What do you see?

What can you smell?

What can you touch?

When you are calm, set an intention.

A Safe Space

Title of space...

Sketch your safe space here	Words that describe your space

Sounds

Sights

Smells

Textures

Who is present

Body Scan

Today's date...........................   Time....................

Where are you?..

Head and Face

Neck and Shoulders

Back

Legs

Chest

Stomach

Arms

Whole body sensations

Sensations

warm – cold – soft – hard – breeze – damp – dry
tense – strong – taut – numb – tingling – tickling – muscle
slender – fragile - pressure – throbbing – blocked – pulse
stabbing – quivering - nauseous – shaking – aching – breathless
wired – anxious - soothed – relaxed – comfortable

Finger Labyrinth

Use your finger to slowly trace a path to the center of the labyrinth

Breathe calmly and slowly as you focus.
When you reach the center, draw a long deep breath or two.

Then trace your path back to the outside
Repeat until you feel more focused and calm.

Focus Words

Breathe - Peace - Relax - Tranquility - Serenity - Calm - Space - Beauty
Love - Wonder - Kindness - Light - Happiness - Joy - Warmth

I WILL
AIM FOR
THE STARS

Self Care Daily Routine

☐ ___________________________

☐ ___________________________

☐ ___________________________

☐ ___________________________

☐ ___________________________

☐ ___________________________

Letting Go of Negative thoughts

We all get negative thoughts - we just need to learn to
change them for positive thoughts.

Negative thought

What triggered this thought?

How did this thought make you feel?

What you might say if a friend expressed these negative thoughts?

What positive thought can you think of to replace the negative one?

Happy Memory Clouds

Fill out these clouds as you think of happy memories.
Use them when your emotions become too much.

What were you doing?

Where were you?

Who was there?

What could you hear?

What could you smell?

Grounding Yourself

What is your name?..

Where are you

Words that describe yur space

Who is with you? What are they doing?

Words that describe your feelings

What do you hear?

What do you see?

What can you smell?

What can you touch?

When you are calm, set an intention.

A Safe Space

Title of space..

Sketch your safe space here	Words that describe your space

Sounds	
Sights	
Smells	
Textures	
Who is present	

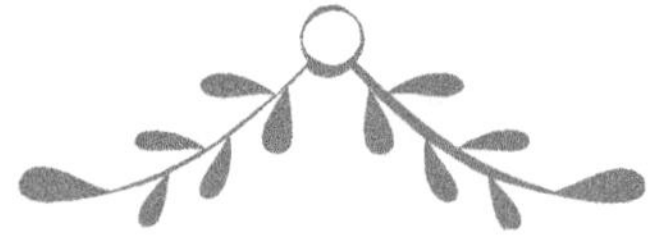

Body Scan

Today's date...........................   Time....................

Where are you?..

Head and Face

Neck and Shoulders

Back

Chest

Stomach

Arms

Legs

Whole body sensations

Sensations

warm – cold – soft – hard – breeze – damp – dry
tense – strong – taut – numb – tingling – tickling – muscle
slender – fragile - pressure – throbbing – blocked – pulse
stabbing – quivering - nauseous – shaking – aching – breathless
wired – anxious - soothed – relaxed – comfortable

Finger Labyrinth

Use your finger to slowly trace a path to the center of the labyrinth

Breathe calmly and slowly as you focus.
When you reach the center, draw a long deep breath or two.

Then trace your path back to the outside
Repeat until you feel more focused and calm.

Focus Words

Breathe - Peace - Relax - Tranquility - Serenity - Calm - Space - Beauty
Love - Wonder - Kindness - Light - Happiness - Joy - Warmth

I AM
BEAUTIFUL
IN MY
OWN WAY

Self Care Daily Routine

Letting Go of Negative thoughts

We all get negative thoughts – we just need to learn to
change them for positive thoughts.

Negative thought

What triggered this thought?

How did this thought make you feel?

What you might say if a friend expressed these negative thoughts?

What positive thought can you think of to replace the negative one?

Happy Memory Clouds

Fill out these clouds as you think of happy memories.
Use them when your emotions become too much.

What were you doing?

Where were you?

Who was there?

What could you hear?

What could you smell?

Grounding Yourself

What is your name?......................................

Where are you

Words that describe yur space

Who is with you? What are they doing?

Words that describe your feelings

What do you hear?

What do you see?

What can you smell?

What can you touch?

When you are calm, set an intention.

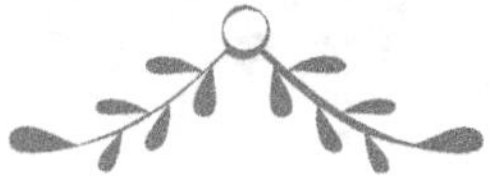

A Safe Space

Title of space..

Sketch your safe space here	Words that describe your space

Sounds	
Sights	
Smells	
Textures	
Who is present	

Body Scan

Today's date..........................   Time...................

Where are you?...

Head and Face

Neck and Shoulders

Back

Chest

Stomach

Arms

Legs

Whole body sensations

Sensations

warm – cold – soft – hard – breeze – damp – dry
tense – strong – taut – numb – tingling – tickling – muscle
slender – fragile - pressure – throbbing – blocked – pulse
stabbing – quivering - nauseous – shaking – aching – breathless
wired – anxious - soothed – relaxed – comfortable

Finger Labyrinth

Use your finger to slowly trace a path to the center of the labyrinth

Breathe calmly and slowly as you focus.
When you reach the center, draw a long deep breath or two.

Then trace your path back to the outside
Repeat until you feel more focused and calm.

Focus Words

Breathe - Peace - Relax - Tranquility - Serenity - Calm - Space - Beauty
Love - Wonder - Kindness - Light - Happiness - Joy - Warmth

I AM
SMART

Self Care Daily Routine

Letting Go of Negative thoughts

We all get negative thoughts – we just need to learn to
change them for positive thoughts.

Negative thought

What triggered this thought?

How did this thought make you feel?

What you might say if a friend expressed these negative thoughts?

What positive thought can you think of to replace the negative one?

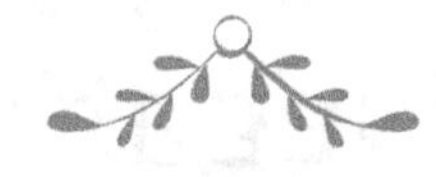

Happy Memory Clouds

Fill out these clouds as you think of happy memories.
Use them when your emotions become too much.

What were you doing?

Where were you?

Who was there?

What could you hear?

What could you smell?

Grounding Yourself

What is your name?.......................................

Where are you

Words that describe yur space

Who is with you? What are they doing?

Words that describe your feelings

What do you hear?

What do you see?

What can you smell?

What can you touch?

When you are calm, set an intention.

A Safe Space

Title of space..

Sketch your safe space here	Words that describe your space

Sounds	
Sights	
Smells	
Textures	
Who is present	

Body Scan

Today's date......................... Time...................

Where are you?...

Head and Face

Neck and Shoulders

Back

Legs

Chest

Stomach

Arms

Whole body sensations

Sensations

warm – cold – soft – hard – breeze – damp – dry
tense – strong – taut – numb – tingling – tickling – muscle
slender – fragile - pressure – throbbing – blocked – pulse
stabbing – quivering - nauseous – shaking – aching – breathless
wired – anxious - soothed – relaxed – comfortable

Finger Labyrinth

Use your finger to slowly trace a path to the center of the labyrinth

Breathe calmly and slowly as you focus.
When you reach the center, draw a long deep breath or two.

Then trace your path back to the outside
Repeat until you feel more focused and calm.

Focus Words

Breathe - Peace - Relax - Tranquility - Serenity - Calm - Space - Beauty
Love - Wonder - Kindness - Light - Happiness - Joy - Warmth

I AM
IMPORTANT

Self Care Daily Routine

- [ ] ______________________________
- [ ] ______________________________
- [ ] ______________________________
- [ ] ______________________________
- [ ] ______________________________
- [ ] ______________________________

Letting Go of Negative thoughts

We all get negative thoughts - we just need to learn to
change them for positive thoughts.

Negative thought

What triggered this thought?

How did this thought make you feel?

What you might say if a friend expressed these negative thoughts?

What positive thought can you think of to replace the negative one?

Happy Memory Clouds

Fill out these clouds as you think of happy memories.
Use them when your emotions become too much.

What were you doing?

Where were you?

Who was there?

What could you hear?

What could you smell?

Grounding Yourself

What is your name?..

Where are you

Words that describe yur space

Who is with you? What are they doing?

Words that describe your feelings

What do you hear?

What do you see?

What can you smell?

What can you touch?

When you are calm, set an intention.

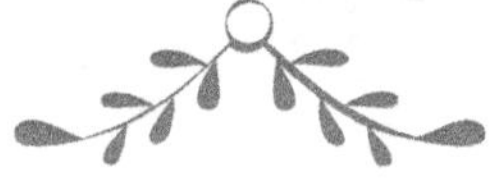 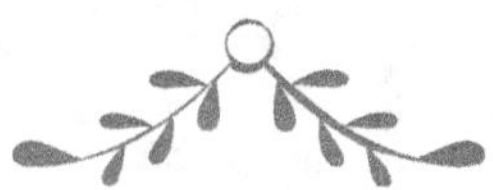

A Safe Space

Title of space...

Sketch your safe space here   Words that describe your space

Sounds

Sights

Smells

Textures

Who is present

Body Scan

Today's date................................   Time....................

Where are you?..

Head and Face

Chest

Neck and Shoulders

Stomach

Back

Arms

Legs

Whole body sensations

Sensations

warm – cold – soft – hard – breeze – damp – dry
tense – strong – taut – numb – tingling – tickling – muscle
slender – fragile - pressure – throbbing – blocked – pulse
stabbing – quivering - nauseous – shaking – aching – breathless
wired – anxious - soothed – relaxed – comfortable

Finger Labyrinth

Use your finger to slowly trace a path to the center of the labyrinth

Breathe calmly and slowly as you focus.
When you reach the center, draw a long deep breath or two.

Then trace your path back to the outside
Repeat until you feel more focused and calm.

Focus Words

Breathe - Peace - Relax - Tranquility - Serenity - Calm - Space - Beauty
Love - Wonder - Kindness - Light - Happiness - Joy - Warmth